CHEROKEE

I·N·S·I·D·E
ITALY

Ian James

Photography: Chris Fairclough

Franklin Watts
London · New York · Sydney · Toronto

CONTENTS

1988 Franklin Watts
12a Golden Square
London W1

Published in the USA by
Franklin Watts Inc.
387 Park Avenue South
New York, N.Y. 10016

Franklin Watts Australia
14 Mars Road
Lane Cove
NSW 2066

Design: Edward Kinsey
Illustrations: Hayward Art Group

UK ISBN: 0 86313 711 3
US ISBN: 0-531-10613-6
Library of Congress Catalog
Card Number: 88-50193

Phototypeset by Lineage, Watford
Printed in Belgium

Additional Photographs:
Allsport 19, Zoe Dominic 22 (T);
Italian State Tourist Office 5 (T), 21, 22;
Mansell Collection 8; Popperfoto 9

Front cover: Chris Fairclough
Back cover: Chris Fairclough

The land

Italy is a large country in southern Europe. It consists mainly of a peninsula, a long land mass shaped like a boot, which is surrounded by arms of the Mediterranean Sea. Italy also includes two large, mainly mountainous islands – Sicily and Sardinia – and several small ones.

Mountains and hills cover four-fifths of Italy. The highest mountains are the Alps in the north. The tallest peak is Mont Blanc, which rises 4,807 m (15,771 ft) on Italy's border with France. The Alps contain many beautiful lakes.

Many rivers flow from the Alps into Italy's largest lowland, the mainly flat Po Valley. The Po, which is 670 km (416 miles) long, is Italy's longest river. It flows across northern Italy into the Adriatic Sea.

Below: **Italy's Mediterranean Coast has many attractive beaches and resorts.**

Above: **Mount Vesuvius, a volcano in southern Italy, overlooks Naples.**

Left: **The Dolomites in northeastern Italy are part of the Alps.**

South of the Po valley are the Apennine mountains. This range forms the backbone of the Italian peninsula. It contains some flat basins, but it is mainly rugged country.

A chain of volcanoes runs though southern Italy. It includes Vesuvius near Naples, the small, volcanic Lipari Islands and Mount Etna in Sicily. Vesuvius erupted with great force in AD79 and destroyed two towns, Herculaneum and Pompeil. Vesuvius last erupted in 1944. Etna erupts more frequently than Vesuvius.

The mountains of northern Italy have cold, snowy winters and sunny summers, and plenty of rain throughout the year. In the south, summers are dry and hot, with occasional thunderstorms. Winters are mild and moist.

Above: **Lake d'Orta is one of several beautiful lakes in northern Italy.**

The people and their history

Throughout history, many people, including Greeks, Phoenicians, Gauls and Normans, have settled in Italy. One early group, the Etruscans, who probably came from the east, founded a civilization in central Italy.

Etruscan kings once ruled Rome. But the Romans overthrew the Etruscans in 509BC and made Rome a republic. The Romans conquered a large empire, including about a quarter of Europe and parts of North Africa and the Middle East. They brought law and order to the conquered peoples. Ruins of great Roman cities, temples, roads and bridges can be seen throughout Italy.

The Roman Empire finally ended in AD476, when Germanic tribes defeated the last Roman emperor, Romulus Augustulus.

Below: **The ancient ruins of the Forum in Rome that was the heart of government during the Roman Empire.**

For most of the time after the fall of the Roman Empire, Italy was divided into small states or it was ruled by foreign powers. Some city-states, such as Florence and Venice, achieved great wealth. In the 14th and 15th centuries, they helped artists who led a great artistic movement called the Renaissance.

Spain, Austria and France all ruled Italy for periods between the 16th and 19th centuries. Most of Italy was united in 1861, largely through the efforts of a patriot, Giuseppe Garibaldi. It became a kingdom under Victor Emmanuel II, former King of Sardinia.

Italy entered World War I in 1915 on the side of the Allies. It gained some land, including the city of Trieste. But the war proved very costly and Italy faced many economic problems in the 1920s.

Below: **The Italian patriot Giuseppe Garibaldi helped Victor Emmanuel (on the white horse) to become King of Italy.**

In 1922, Benito Mussolini, leader of the Italian Fascist movement, became prime minister. From 1925, he ruled as a dictator. Italy entered World War II in 1940 as an ally of Germany. In 1943 the Allies landed in Sicily and Italy surrendered. Soon afterwards, Italy declared war on Germany.

In 1947, the Italians voted to end the monarchy. In 1948, under a new Constitution, Italy became a republic. The Head of State in Italy is the President who serves seven-year terms. The President appoints the prime minister, who heads the government. Italy has many rival political parties. There were 47 governments between 1945 and 1988.

Above: **American troops liberate Rome in 1944. Italians fought alongside the Allied forces for the last 18 months of World War II.**

Towns and cities

Since 1945, many farm workers have left their homes, especially in the poor, dry lands of southern Italy. They now work in cities, especially in the north. Today only 33 per cent of Italians live outside cities and towns. The Po valley is Italy's most thickly populated region. The three largest cities in the north are Milan, Turin and Genoa. These cities have many industries. Milan is also a leading commercial city. Genoa is Italy's busiest port.

The other large cities are Rome, the capital, Naples, a seaport, and Palermo, capital of Sicily. Many cities are old. Their ancient ruins, beautiful old palaces and churches are tourist attractions. But their narrow streets are often filled with noisy traffic. Pollution caused by car exhaust gases is common.

Below: **Many farmers live in small farming villages near their farms.**

Left: **The Leaning Tower of Pisa. Italy has many historic cities which attract vast numbers of tourists.**

Below: **Italian cities are linked by an excellent system of high-speed roads.**

Some of Italy's towns and cities were once even more important than they are today. Some, such as Bologna, Florence, Genoa, Milan, Pisa and Venice, were the capitals of powerful city-states. Some were capitals of large kingdoms. For example, Naples, which was an ancient Greek colony before it became a Roman town in 326BC, was capital of a country called the Kingdom of the Two Sicilies from 1734 until it became part of the Kingdom of Italy in 1861.

One of Italy,s most beautiful cities is Venice. It stands on a group of islands in a coastal lagoon in northeastern Italy. Venice has canals instead of streets. Many people travel around in gondolas (long, flat-bottomed boats) or motorboats instead of buses. Venice has magnificent churches, such as St. Mark's Cathedral, palaces and many art treasures.

Below: **The beautiful city of Venice is built on islands in a lagoon by the sea.**

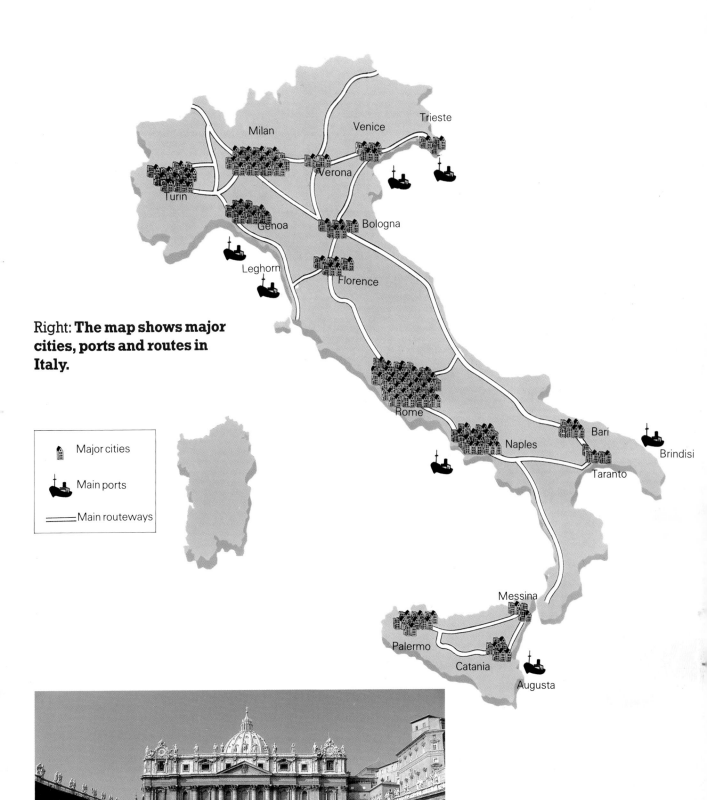

Right: **The map shows major cities, ports and routes in Italy.**

Trieste
Milan
Venice
Verona
Turin
Genoa
Bologna
Leghorn
Florence
Rome
Naples
Bari
Brindisi
Taranto
Messina
Palermo
Catania
Augusta

Major cities

Main ports

Main routeways

Left: **St Peter's Church is in Vatican City, a tiny state in the city of Rome.**

13

Rome became capital of Italy in 1870. But this beautiful city, which stands on the Tiber River about 25 km (16 miles) from the sea, is often called the Eternal City, because it has been a heart of civilization for more than 2,000 years. Central Rome contains impressive ruins, including the Forum, from which the Roman Empire was ruled, and the huge Colosseum.

Rome has many fine churches. The best known is St. Peter's in Vatican City. Vatican City, the headquarters of the Roman Catholic Church, is the World's smallest independent nation. It covers an area of only 44 hectares (108.7 acres) in northwestern Rome.

Most people in Rome have jobs in commerce, government and other services. Only one in five works in industries.

Below: **The plan of Rome shows some of its famous buildings, streets and squares.**

1 **St. Peter's Church**
2 **Castel Sant' Angelo (a Medieval fortress)**
3 **Piazza Navona**
4 **Palazzo Farnese**
5 **The Pantheon**
6 **Piazza di Spagna and Spanish Steps**
7 **Via Vittorio Veneto**
8 **Ancient Roman ruins**
9 **The Colosseum**

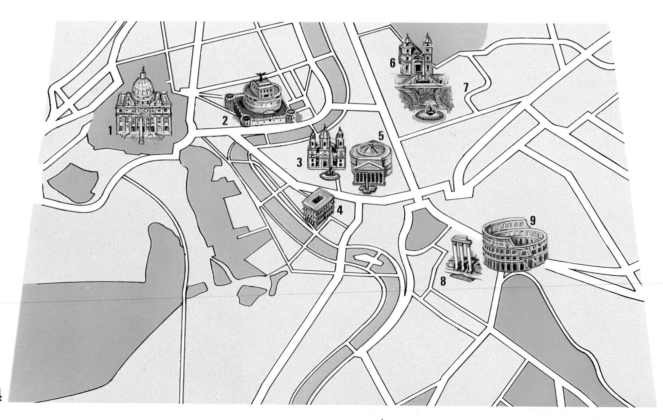

Family life

Two-thirds of Italian families own their homes.
Many city people live in apartments. But there
are plenty of modern houses with gardens in
the suburbs. In recent years, living standards
have risen. By 1988, 76 out of every 100 Italian
households owned a car. Home furnishings
have improved greatly and four out of every
five households have a washing machine.

Families in rural areas are generally less
prosperous. The average income in Italy south
of Rome is less than three-fifths of that in
central and northern Italy. Unemployment is
also twice as high in the south.

Family life is valued highly by most Italians,
who keep in close contact with their relatives.
Many families enjoy entertaining their
relatives and friends at home.

Left: **A family outside their
apartment block in Turin.**

Left: **Most Italian apartments have balconies where people can dry their laundry.**

Below: **An Italian family in the living room.**

Food

Each region of Italy has its own special dishes. For example, pizza, which is now popular throughout the world, originally came from Naples. Bologna is known for its sausages, Parma for its smoked ham and Milan for the thick soup, minestrone. Italy is famous for its pasta, including lasagne, macaroni, spaghetti and vermicelli. Pasta, which is made from flour, is often eaten as a first course, followed by a meat dish or salad, and a dessert or fruit.

Breakfast for most people consists of a roll and coffee. Lunch is usually the main meal, while dinner is a lighter meal. Many Italians drink wine with their lunch and dinner, though mineral water is also popular. Famous Italian wines include Chianti, Frascati, Marsala, Soave and Valpolicella.

Below: **Many people shop in open-air markets or small shops.**

Above: **Meals are important family occasions.**

Left: **Mixed pasta dishes are often served as the first course of a meal.**

Sports and pastimes

The most popular spectator sport is soccer, which attracts large crowds on Sundays. Another major sporting event is the Tour of Italy bicycle race, which lasts about three weeks. Motor racing is also popular. The race track at Monza, near Naples, is used for the Italian Grand Prix.

Fishing, horse riding, hunting and tennis are other leading sports, while the ski slopes in the Alps and Apennines attract people from December to May.

More than 90 per cent of Italian homes have a television set. Television viewing is the most popular pastime, followed by reading and going to the movies. About two out of every five Italians take their annual holiday away from home, mainly at seaside resorts. Few Italians go abroad for their holidays.

Below: **Italy's leading soccer teams attract great loyalty from their spectators.**

Left: **Skiing has become a popular winter sport.**

Below: **On Sundays many people relax by strolling through the park.**

The arts

Italy is known for its superb works of art. Some of the world's finest artists, including Leonardo da Vinci (1452-1519), who painted the famous *Mona Lisa*, and Michelangelo (1475-1564), another painter and sculptor of a huge statue of David, were Italians. Leading Italian writers include Dante Alighieri (1265-1321), author of *The Divine Comedy*, and Giovanni Boccaccio (1313-1375), author of *The Decameron*.

Italy is probably even better known as the home of opera, which began in the early 17th century. Such Italian operas as *La Traviata* by Giuseppe Verdi (1813-1901) and *La Bohème* by Giacomo Puccini (1858-1924) are played regularly throughout the world. Italy has produced many great singers.

Below: **Florence is a city of magnificent buildings, churches and museums housing art treasures.**

Above: **A scene from the opera *Aida*, by Verdi, being performed in Verona.**

Left: **The ceiling of the Sistine Chapel in the Vatican was painted by Michelangelo.**

Farming

Farming employs 12 out of every 100 workers in Italy. The main farm region is the Po valley, where wheat, maize and rice are grown. Mulberry leaves are grown to feed silkworms. Cattle are reared in the Po Valley and also on farms in the Alps, which make dairy products. Vines grow on flat terraces on the lower slopes. Italy makes about a fifth of the world's wine.

Grapes are also grown in central and southern Italy. Here the soil is generally poorer than in the north, except for some fertile basins in the Apennine Mountains and near volcanoes, such as in the Bay of Naples.

Almonds, citrus fruits (such as oranges), olives and wheat, are other major crops. Sheep are common. Their milk is used to make cheese.

Below: **Olive groves in Tuscany. Italy is the world's largest producer of olives after Greece.**

23

Above: **A farmer at work in the Po Valley. In the background are grape vines.**

Below: **Italy produces a huge variety of fruits and vegetables both for the home market and export.**

Industry

Italy produces some oil and natural gas. But it has to import both of these fuels and coal to meet its needs. The country has resources of water power. In the 1980s hydroelectric power stations supplied nearly a quarter of Italy's total electricity supply.

Many minerals are mined, but in small quantities. Only mercury and sulphur are produced in sufficient quantities to meet the country's needs. The rest must be imported. Because many materials are imported, many of Italy's factories are found in sea ports, such as Genoa. The country's main industrial region is in the triangle formed by Genoa, Turin and Milan. Industry employs 41 per cent of Italy's workers and manufacturing is Italy's most valuable activity.

Below: **Italy is one of the world's leading producers of cars. They are noted for design.**

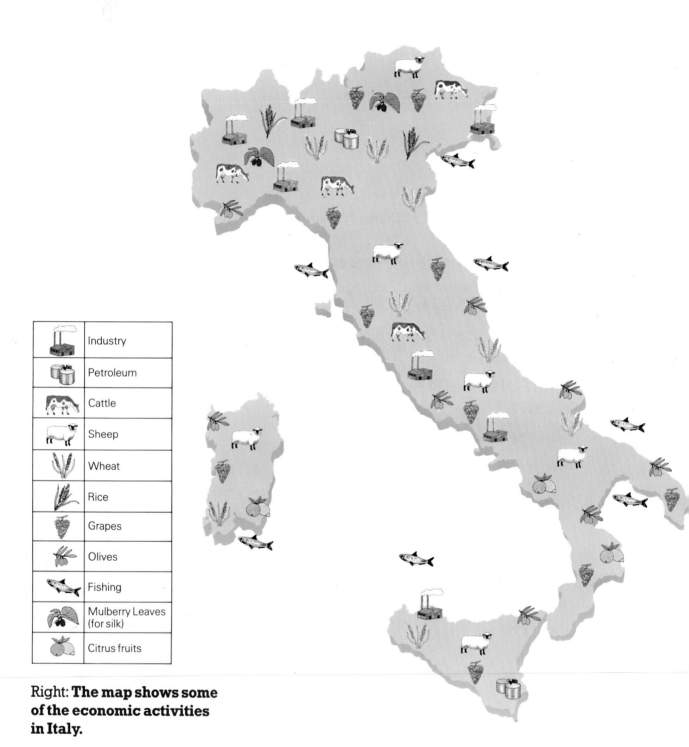

![Industry]	Industry
![Petroleum]	Petroleum
![Cattle]	Cattle
![Sheep]	Sheep
![Wheat]	Wheat
![Rice]	Rice
![Grapes]	Grapes
![Olives]	Olives
![Fishing]	Fishing
![Mulberry Leaves]	Mulberry Leaves (for silk)
![Citrus fruits]	Citrus fruits

**Right: The map shows some
of the economic activities
in Italy.**

Textiles, clothing, leather and footwear are major industrial products. Many items are superbly designed and they are exported. Florence, Milan and Rome are the main cities for the clothing and fashion industry. One famous fashion house, Benneton, is known for its knitwear, which is not too expensive.

Elegant design is important in the success of other industries, including the production of elegant cars. Fiat is Italy's largest privately owned company. It produces not only Fiat cars, but it also owns Alfa Romeo, Autobianchi, Ferrari and Lancia. Italy has many food-processing industries, huge chemical plants and large steel mills. Today, Italy is the world's sixth leading producer of steel and one of the world's top ten industrial countries.

Below: **Italian clothes have a worldwide reputation for quality and design.**

Looking to the future

Italy was a founder member of the European Economic Community, which was established in 1957. It was the poorest of the first six members. But today it is one of the four richest nations in the 12-nation Community, along with West Germany, France and Britain.

Only a few years ago, Italy was called the "sick man of the European Community." It suffered from political instability and terrorism throughout most of the 1960s and 1970s. In the 1980s, however it made great strides. By the late 1980s, its industries were booming and political instability seemed to be a thing of the past. As a result, the tourist industry was continuing to grow and living standards for most people were rising sharply.

Below: **A school in Turin. Italians can now look forward to a bright future.**

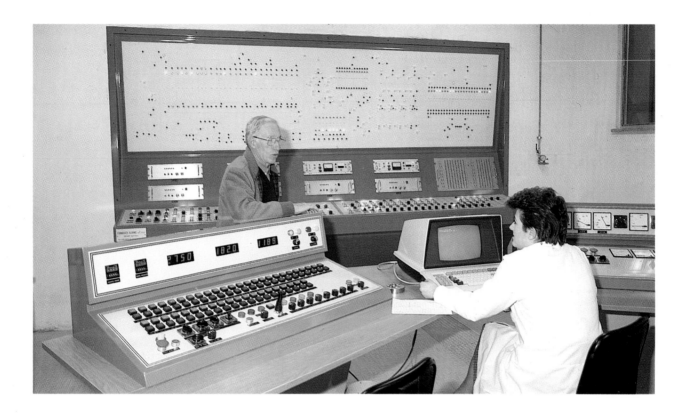

Despite its successes, Italy still faces many problems. Poverty still exists, especially in the south. The development of industry has also led to pollution, especially around the cities and factory areas.

Italy is also facing similar problems to other western industrial countries. For example, its population is ageing and drug addiction is becoming more common. Italy also has a large "black economy." This means that large numbers of people get income from jobs (often second jobs) on which they do not pay taxes. However, some people think that the large "black economy" is a good sign, showing that the people are enterprising. Another important sign for the future is the growth of new high-technology industries.

Above: **Italy has many high-technology industries.**

Facts about Italy

Area:
301,225 sq km
(116,304 sq miles)

Population:
57,350,850 (1987 est)

Capital:
Rome

Largest cities:
Rome (pop 2,826,000)
Milan (1,515,000)
Naples (1,206,000)
Turin (1,035,000)
Genoa (736,000)
Palermo (720,000)

Official language:
Italian

Religion:
Christianity

Main exports:
Textiles, chemicals,
footwear, iron and steel,
machinery, vehicles

Unit of currency:
Lira

Italy compared with other countries.

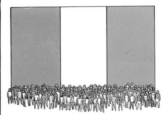
Italy 187 per sq. km.

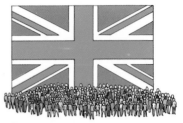
Britain 232 per sq. km.

USA 26 per sq. km.

Australia 2 per sq. km.

Above: **How many people?
Italy is heavily populated
compared with some other
countries.**

Below: **How large? Italy has
a small land area compared
with some countries.**

USA   Australia   Italy   UK

Below: **Italian money and
stamps.**

CZECHOSLOVAKIA

WEST GERMANY

AUSTRIA

HUNGARY

SWITZERLAND

Alps

L. Como

Udine

R. Adige

L. Maggiore

Como

Brescia

Verona

Venice

Trieste

Milan

L. Garda

Padua

N

Turin

Piacenza

R. Po

Genoa

Modena

Ferrara

YUGOSLAVIA

La Spezia

Bologna

Rimini

Pisa

R. Arno

Florence

SAN MARINO

Ancona

Leghorn

Apennines

Ligurian Sea

Elba

Perugia

Adriatic Sea

Terni

Pescara

R. Tiber

CORSICA

Rome

R. Volturno

Foggia

Bari

Sassari

Naples

Vesuvius

R. Bradano

Taranto

SARDINIA

Salerno

Strait of Otranto

Cagliari

Tyrrhenian Sea

Cosenza

Catanzaro

Ionian Sea

0   20   40   60   80 miles

0   40   80   120 km

Palermo

Messina

Reggio

Scale 1:3,215,000

SICILY

Mt Etna

Catania

TUNISIA

Mediterranean Sea

Index

PRINTED IN BELGIUM BY

proost
INTERNATIONAL BOOK PRODUCTION